RIDDLE

FISH HOOK

THORN

KEY

OTHER TITLES FROM AIRLIE PRESS

THE EDDY FENCE   *Donna Henderson*
LAST APPLES OF LATE EMPIRES   *Jessica Lamb*
GARDEN OF BEASTS   *Anita Sullivan*
OUT OF REFUSAL   *Carter McKenzie*
ENTERING   *Cecelia Hagen*
THE NEXT THING ALWAYS BELONGS   *Chris Anderson*
CONGRESS OF STRANGE PEOPLE   *Stephanie Lenox*
IRON STRING   *Annie Lighthart*
STILL LIFE WITH JUDAS & LIGHTNING   *Dawn Diez Willis*
SKEIN OF LIGHT   *Karen McPherson*
PICTURE X   *Tim Shaner*
PARTLY FALLEN   *Deborah Akers*
SETTING THE FIRES   *Darlene Pagán*
THE CATALOG OF BROKEN THINGS   *A. Molotkov*
WISH MEAL   *Tim Whitsel*
BORN   *Jon Boisvert*

RIDDLE

FISH HOOK

THORN

KEY

KELLY TERWILLIGER

Airlie Press
PORTLAND OREGON
2017

Airlie Press is supported by book sales, by contributions to the press from its supporters, and by the work donated by all the poet-editors of the press.

Airlie Press
PORTLAND OREGON

P.O. BOX 82653
PORTLAND OR 97282
WWW.AIRLIEPRESS.ORG

EMAIL: EDITORS@AIRLIEPRESS.ORG

Copyright © 2017 Kelly Terwilliger

All Rights Reserved. No part of this book may be reproduced in whole or in part without the written permission of the publisher except in the context of reviews or critical writing.

Cover and Book Design: Beth Ford, Glib Communications & Design

First Edition
ISBN: 978-0-9895799-6-4
Library of Congress Control Number: 2017947955

Printed in the United States of America

*for Leo*

## ONE — AIR

- 3  WHEN THE NTH TERM IS INFINITE
- 4  THE OPPOSITE OF GHOSTS
- 5  HANDKERCHIEF
- 6  IF X EQUALS X
- 7  UNDER THE PILLOW
- 8  THE HILLSIDE
- 9  FROZEN SHIRT
- 10 FALL
- 12 MY MOTHER'S FOX
- 13 HARD RIVER
- 14 NIGHT SONG
- 15 WHAT IF
- 16 CANYON DEL MUERTO

## TWO — BODY

- 19 STRANGE COAT
- 20 SNOW GLOBE
- 21 GIFT HORSE
- 22 BEGINNING WITH SONS
- 24 UPON FINDING THE OLD CALENDAR MATCHES THE COMING YEAR
- 26 SPOONS
- 27 REMEMBERING
- 28 ROSE GARDEN
- 29 SWIMMING BEHIND THE HOSPITAL
- 30 ALMOST VENICE
- 31 INCOMING

## THREE — SOME WAY IN

35 THE UNDERSIDE OF ISLANDS

36 SITTING ON THE CROSSPIECE OF A SPANISH H

38 DAYS I'VE LET PASS BY

39 WHAT STORY

40 WET HORSES

41 GOODNIGHT GORILLA

42 OVER JOE NEY SLOUGH

44 LANDSCAPE

46 EACH OF US IN THE DOORWAY OF OURSELVES

48 IMMORTALS

## FOUR — THE LOWER WING

53 NET, SORROW, CRADLE

54 WHISTLING BEETHOVEN

55 IN THE MIDDLE OF SINGING

56 AROUND THE WORLD

58 MUSEUM OF ART

60 BEYOND SWANS

62 POST OFFICE IN DECEMBER

64 IN THE BRIEF KINGDOM OF ICE

65 SOME WINTER

66 SWING SONG

67 LETTING GO

68 ABATEMENT

70 SOUNDING

72 FLOAT

74 IT'S BEEN A LONG TIME SINCE I TALKED WITH A MOUNTAIN

76 BLOOMING

## ONE ~ AIR

## WHEN THE NTH TERM IS INFINITE

Air crackles like cold
fins swimming currents of quickening
dark. Under ice
my imagined
sighs. Blowhole.
Stars.

In ordinary hours I have given names
to the long-legged flying ones
that appear in my house
and rest on the walls.
I have named the casual deer, their various children.
The vole that keeps dying
and reappearing.

But the door that blows open
to the sound of rain: what is its name?
Louder now, drumming
on the tin roof of my tongue. A song
under the night garage.
The gravel, the woodpile, the rope swing.
The blue canoe floating forever
upside-down.

The roar of the rain. I have
no name for this. No name
for myself.

The air trembles. And sometimes—
opens.

Stubborn rind. Peel it back,
gently, lift it... what is there? What is
there—
*Say it—*

## THE OPPOSITE OF GHOSTS

The river is a fish on its way somewhere,
long body brushing rocks.
It rushes by, horse, chariot, bright

water galloping under flotillas of ice
festooned with birds preening
as their rafts swirl
and ease to disappear beneath them.

In the distance, a bridge curves
the way sky bends
over water

to a mat of ground just clear of snow:
soggy grass, and trees
half in dream stand bare,
churring with blackbirds, red epaulets gleaming, eyes
cocked to the sun.

One tree whirs. Dry seeds, winter-clung
shiver. No leaves.
No sign of buds. Just
the opposite of ghosts:
every branch an imagined profusion.
Bright dazzle
of not-yet here.

## HANDKERCHIEF

Floating word, an artifact
I'd forgotten—
a father, who sneezed and carried
this crumpled peony in his pocket

*eyes watering, a burst like a horse
stamping in its stall, and the quiet after*

*caught in a shaft of yellow light—*

       *             *

*He had a good heart. He had
a bad heart.* Some things have no easy
opposite. The night before he died, he came
round the side of my grandmother's house in her dream,
a boy again. Knobby knees. Cotton shorts.
The worry line she knew between his eyes.

We scatter
in pieces of being. Each facet complete
until someone opens the midnight door
and pulls another scrap onto the carpet. Bewildered
mooncalf blinking, pink nostrils wet,
bell around its shaggy neck
ringing beside familiar sofa and chairs.
*Once upon a time,*

I folded my father's handkerchiefs,
warm from the dryer, clinging together
like pages of a fragile book.
Thin, like air—I loved
how easy they were to fold: soft square
halving and halving. What if I'd just kept going?
Blossoms unblooming, reversing
to a single point
with everything inside them.

IF X EQUALS X

*Even the smallest thing has something in it which is unknown.*
—Gustave Flaubert

Perhaps Flaubert's window was open
a crack, left by the housekeeper
to freshen the room, freshly
dusted when she was struck
by the thought of someone she'd left
waiting on the other side of town.

A new wedge of light
lit where the window tilted
when the writer entered later—
the sky could spill in, was spilling
winter's light feet and the ghosts
of something akin to spring,

that slim knife of whiteness, the glinting
difference between open and shut,
between *still*, and what it means
when one finger still lifts,

when one sound shifts in a word
and summons another world

in which wrestlers crouch
on the mat and wait for the whistle:
you can look into their eyes
dark as knotholes and they will not look out.

They are listening
to the weight of air around them. They wait
for the touch, the plunge
into sand and wax and fur,
strange teeth of sinews as they lunge and fall
and writhe away to aim again

for the throat,
the idea of throat, opponent,
self, all that one conquers, betrays, turns,
and returns to. Close. Closer.

## UNDER THE PILLOW

A ribbon, a cough, a whale's tooth. The book
I meant to open. A nest
     of turtle's eggs
     buried in the sand
waiting for the sun to call them
down the long
beach of my bed to the sea in the dark
beyond me.
     Galaxy, machine, mind
twinkling, breathing, like night spread over
the harbor that once harbored me.

     Fog makes white blossoms
     out of anything bright
     and covers your face like a veil.

     Boats rock their loose
     ropes, and winches jangle in voices
     talking themselves to sleep

     under my pillow
the sea sighs
unrolls, pulls back again. My father folds
the clothes he wasn't buried in.
     My grandmother rustles, a bird
     in the kitchen that would be yellow
if any light were lit. She waits for the coffee pot to mutter.

Who knows what she thinks when she is alone
in the rooms of my mind.
The door is open.
The lost things come and go as they please.

## THE HILLSIDE

Shadows recline long
and lazy. It could be dozing
anywhere.

Who feels the breathing,
and feels sure?

*The whole hillside lies with one eye open.*

Not that it watches for me.
Not that I will ever find that eye. Not that I am
that eye. A tree shifts, slightly. The wind
lifts a loop of vine.

The river curves away,
the drying trees stand open.

And if I hold my breath?
The sky goes on unreading itself
in threads of cloud.

## FROZEN SHIRT

I'd lost my
spark, my map's
curious tongue, I wasn't brave when
bright, unbearable, I
brought the frozen shirt inside.

Stiff: not cardboard, not heavy
paper, but more like it had been
alive. Now matted. Dried wrack
above the tide. And I loved
its lift: not empty. Not full, but a sail
arrested in taut gesture, armlessly bowing
or maybe doubled over,

laughing. I hold my hide
between my fingertips.
I wave around my blue skinself,
a piece of absolute
until it melts.

      Rain, my amanuensis,
rattles away, dissolving as it writes.
Never mind. Let's just put in the bit
about jumping into the sea, not how long it took
to hold back fear, but that I did it:
funneling down through the long, long silk
chemise of air, longer than I'd ever dared
to plummet
and how entering
was like falling through a parachute
of strange wet arms
that stopped me, saved me, pulled me
all to pieces. Light and water and limbs
in a great seethe of froth and broken blue,
clashing until I rose and the bright
surface opened. My lip, torn,
inside where no one could see,
when I tasted that red
and secret salt of me.

FALL

In shagbark hickories they run and leap
high where the branches begin to bend

or so I saw them in my mind.
My uncle said *they have tough skins,
not like rabbits.* He said
*the fox is bigger than the grey and
not so fast. They'll sit and peer even as you aim.*
He said he told a guest once, sure,
they were eating chicken, tree chicken,
   and he chuckled. He didn't say *hunger*
just that

*going into woods you have to know
how to wait* for a kind of quiet,
to let it fill with subtle sounds.
You have to let
   the world resume
as if you weren't there.

Coming home from hunting
he was always most awake, his mind
clear, trailing the blunt eager
smell of broken twigs.

After he'd gone I found a piece of ginger root
forgotten, shriveled
to a dried squirrel's paw.
   Could you wear a ginger foot
    to ward off hesitation? If you needed?

There's a tumbling
down from spangled branches. Old mansions
    through which a body
    falls
      and falls, tail trailing last.
If you're quick, you can catch them before they hit.
They never have to touch the ground
    if you catch them in your hands, soft. Still warm.

MY MOTHER'S FOX

She saw it once, on the road
of her childhood where the pond and the woods
curved away. At the shadow's edge,
an exclamation point—

leftover grasses whisking

and I can't remember exactly how or if
she described it—
the air between us rubbed clean by crickets,
the sky already blowing leaves
over the stones we'd come to sit on.

*There*, she always said. *That's where.*
And every time I passed thereafter
I looked, in case, into the space still waiting
for the fox to come again, an emptiness

having shaped, once, a small red
thought, a white-tipped brush,
a sharp quick jump over the lazy
dog of late September, this

dart of *yes*
pulled from her landscape,
put into mine.

HARD RIVER

The photograph is the kind usually discarded
because the child you wanted to save forever
looked away just then.

He was throwing a rock into the river.
His body turned to follow what happened next.
A little splash.

The current drives beyond him
fast and drowned with rocks dragged down the glacial valleys.

But his hair floats in the sun.
You could put your hand into its whispery fuzz.
If you sat down, he'd climb right into your lap,
he'd lean against you, because he is ready
for anyone's kindness.

What does he know? Round baby fingers
curl as the rock disappears. The distant sun rests
briefly warm on bare legs

and the rocks, ancient and loose. Everything ancient
and loose. Who belongs in a place like this?

Someone said *Watch!* and *Here, try!*
And he did, his awkward throw, the river
rushing so fast it could sweep him away like a fly—

Can you see how the picture needs him? The child's soft
      blur, the effortless
trust in a landscape that doesn't care if it's trusted or not—

the clamoring, the roar of the river, the wordless roar.

NIGHT SONG

See my scrappy sticks? Limbs of letters I toss into the air
to see what happens, what might be,
to watch them whickering down, like the notes
      of the owl who called all night
outside my window. Not sorrow, but the overflow
of wanting to live, to break open
all those feathers
into night, its nestle, its infinitude
wanting to fill the vast gap as I did without meaning to

the night we drove late onto the flat belly
of a desert I'd never seen by day.
I conjured trees and hills at every curve in the road.
Obscure, the land kept rising up. I sent forests
over all the imagined horizons, out of my wandering mind
that knew what it knew.

Oh, I know wanting to throw
a vestige of singing again and again
down those dark stairs! Bird I can't feel,
trees I can't see—

When the road stopped
we threw our blankets on the ground, still
knowing nothing. A blade of wind
swishing the cold above our faces
like a boy flicks a thin stick
just to hear the quick of it, the sharp whisper,
so far away, so intimate
it hurts.

# WHAT IF

I wait to feel the feet
of the angel of confusion, the one
who runs through heaven and hell
with no shoes on.
Pitter patter touching down
on the center of the sternum,
bridge of bone between weight
and light.

There will be a commotion of
wings, the still air not still, until I
understand loneliness
the way water does,
each incarnation
being only what holds around it.

But I won't say goodbye! Just give me
hello, and hello. Wings descending, the air
parting, and closing,
and opening again. Whatever I have loved
scribbling and singing, not far away.

Angel of hidden things, hold on to me
with your handkerchief of wind.
I thought I wanted simplicity,
but the voice of alchemy and chance
keeps turning me around.

Angel of precipices, washing away
the colors of the world. I say
*write your name on my arm so I don't forget,*
your feathers too soft to pronounce.

I want the angel of howling to nod.
To give the okay. The sky to be ready.
*What if you told a story* asked the child
*about someone who had eyes all over their body?*
Everywhere, blinking...

## CANYON DEL MUERTO

The horses are small
under the yellow.
Under the tree.

They could be thoughts
I put there. Their glossy curves,
their shadows.

Did they move, and then hold still?
Or did I fill them
with breathing, ears flicking—

the tree-thought rising from them
a cloud
of gold, a swarm

of papered wings
made for soaking up light. Each leaf
precise

but seeming to blur,
to mingle with air
and dying, the day
caught

at the edge of abeyance.

TWO BODY

## STRANGE COAT

Sometimes a whale will die at sea
and its body remains
a lost balloon
afloat, rising and falling,
turning softly within
to something like cream, until
the skin splits, the rest
falls away.

What then, strange coat, washed ashore?
Bewildering softness, traces,
the blowhole's empty portal.
A hill of skin,
enough to hide a house.

This is what we find.
A man rides his horse down the beach,
toward all of us waiting,
the clouds so low his head skims them, his hat
pulls them into plumes.
We stand in the deep wind,
waiting for him to arrive.

But out at sea the bones are still falling.
I'm sure of it. Slipped from the skin
they descend through the sea's green rooms,
huge bones made small by distance and depth
slowly spiraling down.

SNOW GLOBE

Something shakes the crabapple tree
the one now drenched in blossoms—

    Before, I stood ankle deep
in wet grass gone slick as ink

looking in, the kitchen window a glass lamp glowing,
and in the lamp, the small room surrounding

the strewn table and my father
in his flannel shirt.

    He's idly running
    his hand through his hair.

    He's humming, reading,
    not looking up.

This was another time.
Or this was a dream. The grass is black,
the damp yard cooling fast from the day,

the rinsing notes of thrushes
in the flock of alders
that rustled for years down the hill.

    If he looked this way he'd see himself,
    wavering in double panes, a hint
    of trees against the drained sky,

the window like water between us.

I'd like to shake that lit room, wrench those papers loose,
send them whirling the way you must
to wake a scene that sleeps.

Too low, the ceiling! Let's take the roof off
    so the falling petals last longer—

This brief snowy drift

time's only passage here, and I
the ghost pressed up against it.

GIFT HORSE

*You come to a house made of bones*
      *You come to a house made of feathers and hair*
      *You come to a house made of teeth and nails*
      *In search of know-not-what from know-not-where.*

A horse on the beach today,
like an old sail blown in.

The teeth give it away.

And the wind can't leave it alone, keeps plucking
the sand's wet sleeve,

as if bringing it to me
to show: *see?* As if I hadn't seen, and tried to look away.

      *As if swimming in sleep, hooves drifting*
    *tail swirling like seaweed.*

Tufts and clumps are everywhere.
The line between beach and disaster grows slim.

It arrived with the tide. It became
the length of the beach.
From jetty to rock I walk its body.

Now the wind picks up.
Bits of dry hair,
the damp horsehair, the sea-damp sand, everything
becomes kin, and strange.
*There was a house of bones, a house of hair, a house of teeth—*

I begin to wear fur. I feel hairs on my skin,
between my teeth, in every breath.

If I put my hand into the horse's mouth
and reach behind the sand, behind the tongue
that isn't there, something jiggles.
      *Riddle, fish hook, thorn, key—*

BEGINNING WITH SONS

Sometimes they bring home crosswords, and we do them,
or I do them, a kind of devotion
as they lie on the floor with their papers and books.
One page missing from the math book.
Why tear a page from a book of math?

*Fever, or favorite numbers. To wrap the fish, to start the fire.*
*The night was a cold one*
*and the stars were their own equations.*

They study. I read
about an ancient scroll
covered with practical calculations:
how to divide ten gallons of animal fat
to get you through the year, how to find
the area of a distant sphere.

The page begins, brazen with confidence:
"The correct method of reckoning, for grasping
the meaning of things, and knowing
everything—obscurities and all secrets—"

such as when your sons begin to resemble your father.
If you stand at Y, is the trajectory always loss?

*When Echo looked up all she had were leftover*
*pieces already said.*
*She had to find the ends and try them on*
*as beginnings.*

Once before they were born I walked out
across a frozen lake, each step
creaking and sighing and the wind
shuffling beside me like an old man. The ice
was absolute, pocked and ridged. Pieces of voices
came back in the broken air. I could have gone on,
dusk coming round my shoulders like a heavy coat
left all night in the frozen cab of a parked truck,
but I stopped, and turned,
somewhere indistinguishable from anywhere else, dry snow
pooling in eddies around my feet.
I went home. Distant motors gunning, the lid of cold
clapping down, and mystery
stretching out like strings of flags and shadows.

## UPON FINDING THE OLD CALENDAR MATCHES THE COMING YEAR

In the game where all the floor was lava
you had to make your way across a room
without ever touching down: couch, chair, coffee table, cushion.

Then the sky descended and erased what came before.
Daffodils filled
the afterward rooms. White,
then yellow. Erased? Or altered.
      I found a calendar
      of the year before my father died. It exactly fits
the year I'm about to enter. I will be the age he was.

The little hairs of me
rise, they urge: go back, go somewhere else—

Today I met a man who plays the tuba.
The horn seemed bigger than he was.
Vessel, silver blossom,
      receptacle, mouth.
You have to be willing
to take up more space than you fill,
like when I lived alone with the sky
and every night when the Sea Basket closed
I hung that greasy apron on its hook and stepped outside—

He made the sound of wind
blowing through trees. He made the sound of a foghorn at night
calling across that empty parking lot
where the fog hung still and clean
and the soul was vast. So enormous, shining,
you could sit inside it. The summer, the last
of my father's life—
none of us knew it, not even him,
not even when he stepped right out of his body, left it

on the road behind the dune
where you can't see the ocean
but it's everywhere:
the smell, soft roar, the little cries of birds
—he just kept jogging, light, easy,
until he looked back where he'd been
and saw his body in a heap on the ground.

He turned.
Which book explains this? He went back,
he picked himself up, he brought himself home to tell us.

There is a slide of time
over time. The ground grows hot underfoot.
        Who do I think I am, walking so close?
To see the wound where the earth has opened itself
breaking and remaking
a long glowing to the edge of the sea.
I walk along the shore in the dark to where the earth
burns and drips
pieces of its molten self into the waves.
Steam and roar and hiss and spray.
And a sound you feel
before you hear it.

SPOONS

Disappearing
under a caul of rain, they rise
in the compost later, glinting, whole

the way the shaman, year after year
is devoured by the bear
then coughed up as bones
which reassemble themselves, growing
more intimate with the souls of things
after each year's digestion.

Spoons, let me wash your bright bodies,
put you into my mouth,
you who have been to the underworld and back.
Beetles, hours, crushed meteors
tangled and dissolved, now
metal on the tongue, a tickle

like the sound of goats, their black and white faces
blinking perpetual surprise, their long ears
listening for the grassy sigh,
ancient, familiar. Let's play, spoons,
something spry, something that laughs and leaves us
with islands of years and the distance
to roam between them, our shirts blowing,
the lush warmth rising.

REMEMBERING

It's putting the pieces
together again, one body,
but whose? You might stand there
thinking, under yourself,
as under a tree, many-limbed and
hairy with moss, the leaves like
golden trumpets poised
to blaze sound, your lungs bright
with breath, and your heart
in its secret room like the eye
of a whale, swimming deep,
the floating world streaming,
the sea shaking in great undulations
the way the flanks of the grand piano
shook under my palms every time
my one-eyed teacher brought Russian composers
roaring back to life. Her twin sat on the couch
under a fog of white hair, smoking cigarettes
until the view outside
disappeared. The music lifted,
its own architecture. The heart of the house
rocked in the wind when November
battered the streaming sea windows
and rimed them with salt
and those rough old hands
scattered themselves over the keys
like leaves in the wind,
like a body falling
to pieces so that it might be
gathered up again.

## ROSE GARDEN

Silly beauty, don't expect me
to admire your appellations:
*Abraham Darby, Albertine,
Altissimo, Anna Maria's
Lovely Daughter.* You of
Clipped Wings, Cossetted
Beds, I will tell you a secret:

You are only real when you
begin to fade.

The river blooms and blooms,
a wild thing, and carries
names away.

So why don't I leave you now,
silly pretty things?

Evening's light is pouring in:
nearby color falls in folds, drinking up light
like honey water. I meant to honor
the lone man facing the river
on the other side of the fence, the way his shoulders
sag into the sound of water rushing through
its spell of rapids. But I sink

into blossoms. Get close enough
and there's nothing else—
color lush as wordless singing, a chorus
rising, complications falling away,
even the sorrows on their little leashes
float
in the reverberating chord.

## SWIMMING BEHIND THE HOSPITAL

Green blackberries on the bank and a black and yellow
snake unlacing the dry grass and
day falling away
        into blue blue clear blue
        the sky's thin goblet rim
        ringing where you rub
        against it

and if you edge down the rocks behind the hospital
the river goes swift, strong enough to carry
a body away
        but kick hard and you'll catch
the rocky wrist of the island laid out in the sun
like a man sleeping, the water rushing
by his arms by his side.

We let ourselves fall into the green muscle
of current and fly with it
        then fight it
crossing onto dry rocks, the sun
leaning over us, the air
thick with eagles and herons folding into gone.

No one stays for long.

But those cool green
arms can hold you. You can go, and glide
and wrestle back to dry light.

Again and again
we climb out and feel new. And the sky
lifts its blue glass. Behind the trees behind us
people lie in their beds
dying, or trying not to.

Let me think of fast water, then—
the slick of blood on my shin, the way my knees have trembled with cold,
        the flying down and coming out again
        into warm summer air.

ALMOST VENICE

All night, I lie awake
over floating streets and listen
to the oracles of things: the voices
of faces in dreams, paving stones,
crumpled paper, bottles, oars.
A bridge
of sudden laughter, a shouted call,
clatter of smoke—

Midnight, and bells
plunge through open blinds,
shaking and ringing the air like a body
of water: I'm in it.
Everything is. Each molecule
shudders with struck sound.

So how can morning arrive
so unruffled? High voices of swallows
and pigeons snapping their wings
like paper fans

when from the recollected window
of a darkened shop a small glass fish comes
floating: flounder
speckled, translucent, a scrap of watered light
alive, as if scooped up
the moment I stepped ashore—

that slick curve, how it might feel
cupped in the palm of my hand.
Glass, not glass, just shining, the moment
before it wriggles away.

INCOMING

A swirl, a skin, a fingerprint
of foam—

the seaweed hour commences:
wet dresses in bunched masses
a mussel shell caught
like a lost canoe, and
little crabs, bubble-drenched
skittering the banks
of islands just invented.

Crisps and clumps
of what has died and dried
line the beach and everywhere
around each curve
of light and stone: water,
its little sound embroidering
the edge of stillness.

The sky's already drifting—
our boat will soon float free—
the rocks rising
slim, slimmer, until
they're loose,

a glimmer underwater.

And we lie, speckled
in sand and shells, elements
repeating themselves
smaller and smaller.

Vanishing, alive—which are we? Which are we most?

Seals rise
through the roof of the sea
to look at land and sky.
They stare, exhaling, nostrils flaring,
then tip their heads up and slip
down the wet chimney
of whoever they are.

THREE　SOME WAY IN

# THE UNDERSIDE OF ISLANDS

Islands sigh and moan in their own languages
as tides spill through their pores

and the skeletons
of boats and planes and guns
sleep under curtains of lagoons.

Now the moon is its own canoe.
Now the fishes swim in the dark,
the birds become shadows on the bodies of trees
and caves of wind and stone
cradle bones where no one finds them.

The fallen skull of a coconut
lies in the cupped hand
of the sand beneath it

and the little crabs in their palaces
quicken over the fallen fruit,
their hungry, whispering feet
searching for some way in.

## SITTING ON THE CROSSPIECE OF A SPANISH H

Of course I want to feel like I belong in the world.
I keep waiting
for something in the landscape to recognize me
but when I name stones, it's only me
pretending they know my name in return.

Sometimes I am eyes. The rest
disappears.
And then, the faded shoe
pressed against the table leg,
this hand here, writing, and here
where the pen meets the page, a secret mind
leaks out, becomes
visible.

I think of the Spanish H. Silent companion in words
that cannot go without it. *Hola. Hablo. Hambre:*
I sit on the crosspiece of a letter that never speaks,
swinging my legs
and water runnels underneath, its syllables waiting
wet as clams.

Every oyster is its own
flounced dress, hard as stone
but it's also the softness within,
which isn't meant to glisten, or come to light.

Strange worlds, our fragile interiors.
Dark rooms, shining like the cave I entered once
in another country. Lights on our foreheads
bobbed as we floated in with the stream—our bodies
disappearing into glinting shadows, looking back
at the daylight of another world.

I went into the throat of a land I didn't know.
Perhaps I didn't belong there.
Or maybe in that moment I became one of its souls.
Who has the truth of any place? Wet stones.
River. Vaulted roof.
Mouth.

## DAYS I'VE LET PASS BY

A woodpecker hung in the trees today
knocking a hollow note.
I didn't say a word.

A white goat nosed out into its yard
as I left the empty house. It called
a tilted question, looking over the fence

but I didn't stop to answer. Late,
when I went out to close the coop
I couldn't see the step and the fallen branch

still lay across the path. But drowsy birds
muttered my approach. All day the world
speaks like this.

## WHAT STORY

What story does he need, the boy
who makes faces when anybody speaks,
lewd beyond his years?

The playground is empty
hours after the school day ends.

There's a lost umbrella
blown inside-out like a flightless
bat, a piece of night torn and thrown
into the path of an unnamed day.

And here's a paper bag
with two ripped holes. Whose
puzzle face?

I say *once upon a time*.
He doesn't blink. I say

*a snowy owl might look just like*
*a grocery sack*
*in the middle of a field.*

Until it turns its head.
Until it opens
in a shudder of snow.

## WET HORSES

Driving home I saw the same wet horses
standing in the rain
like beautiful statues

except they weren't statues. They might have been
hungry. They might have been cold.
Their legs, fringed with earth,
pressed into the heavy muck beneath them.
Ears flicked stillness after each car went by.
The shawling rain, the shag of mud, the whiskered trees
outlasting any passing.

I've let standing horses stand
for dreaming in a still field. I've let them hold
for me a quiet place as I continue on

too busy to linger, but what if,
seeing, I stayed,
let myself fall
into the well of other lungs, secret bellows
sucking in the cold sky, and blowing it out again,
inside the horse's mouth, behind thick teeth,
to hunger's bitter heat? Feel another body's
terrifying heaviness—

It's not that far.

Driving home I see the same wet horses.
I know nothing of horses. Dreams
standing in a field, watching me pick my way through sodden
grasses, watching the warm bucket slosh against my legs,
the towels sway—

*Here,* I'll say. *Easy, now—*

and lift their feet, one by one.

# GOODNIGHT GORILLA

A man who gives up might think
he is leaving the world simpler,
but he sets his beasts
among us. They wander out at twilight
into the fall air, the gates now open,
into a scattering of
leaves, small blown heaps
rustling under displaced paws
with the same dry sounds
they always make this time of year.

And the wind moves through the trees,
a grandfather ruffling the heads
of children bent over books
in which tigers and lions and bears
step out of dreams and walk the streets
and the wind touches their fur
soft, like the fur of rabbits, and also full
of stripes, and tassels
tingling with something like secret
light, a dark light which stays on your hands
after you touch it, and in the story
the animals are never hungry
for more than a little cake. They climb, lonely,
into the zookeeper's bed, wanting only
to be closer to human. We feel them, nestled around us,
breathing, as we breathe.

But now there is no bed.
The beasts lope, they lunge,
into the night where it is raining, hard,
the highway roaring, the rain refracting each beam
into passing chrysanthemums.
Shadows, dodging shadows, climbing higher in the trees.
The shots fired to stop them, before they go too far.
Before they escape what we have imagined them to be.

OVER JOE NEY SLOUGH

I was afraid to look
at his swollen mouth.
I was afraid to look at his eyes.

He was bigger than the other boys
and he smelled like danger.
Mornings when he slouched up
the school bus steps, two stops up the road,
I looked away.
The long arm of the wiper
swung across the face of the bus
and his coat was wet
and rain was all over
his face.

Every day under the dark smudge
of coastal rain—

He closed his eyes during reading, and math.

\*

The day the bus broke down
we could hear gulls screaming
into the wind, only the two of us left
to walk, over the tide pulled back from the flats,
the little scabs of oyster stakes.
Something flew, fast, from under the bridge.

Whatever I said is gone. But he answered:
*I wish I had a different life. I'd like to be*
      *someone else*
           as if a bird
              had fallen from the nest of him
      into my hands—

                \*

When does crushed glass
become sand again? Bird. Scowl. Wound.

Years later, I heard he'd killed a man.
A knife, outside a bar. And I remembered.

There will never be enough room
to stand inside him
without bumping against the walls.

And there I was, all those days,
the smell of desks—chemical, dust, sweat—
blooming damp beneath my cheek
when we put our heads down on our arms,
when the teacher needed a little quiet.

## LANDSCAPE

You could see where horses had been,
droppings heaped like cairns
over pine needles, tiny lines
of criss-cross light.

Maybe these were auspicious signs. But even if
the circles of trees I passed
could enact old pacts and devotions
as they embraced the air between them
would the world be any kinder?

A woman scolds her son
in a low and vicious voice
as soon as we've gone by. Or maybe she's scolding the dog.
Or the sky, or her eyes for what they failed to tell her,
her hands for what they wanted to do.

Brambles scribble over everything
and it's hard to see the world
as more than aftermath, unwanted:
dishwashers, dryers lined up for nowhere,
rusted rows of tractors, a single collapsed box
lying in a ditch. Grassy mounds
rising like graves in a grubby yard,
one lone horse among them, the story

of what's been tossed aside
beginning when no one was looking, or we all
had looked away. Or simply forgot
what started the first altercation. A cow, a well, a wheel,
the smell of cut wood so dense it made the air
shimmer like oil.

A silent raft of crows lifts from devouring
rotting apples, small and wormy.

They watch, wary, until we've gone.
*You didn't need to worry*, we'd say,
if we thought they'd listen.

Fleets of leaves scatter the path.
We crackle over their dry ribs, their last
crisp sounds. Wherever the paved ground buckles,
painted outlines, veined like leaves or bony fishes
cover the wounds to warn us. *Thanks*, we'd say,
if we knew where to say it.

Wanting hangs in the air like
smoke that can't quite rise.
Heaps of smoke, heaping
softly. A man once stood in an
empty field and watched the sun dissolve
frost from everywhere
except beneath his body's shadow.
His neighbor, not wanting to interrupt
what he didn't understand,
left a heap of turnips at the shadow's feet.

I want the gesture that lets you
be more.

The sky dims into late afternoon, the sun
pale behind the clouds, a glinting dime
like the one I found by the creek where we stopped
just before turning back. Silver eye above the rubble
of river cobbles. Pick up any rock from a pile and set it
anywhere, on purpose. It changes.
Chosen, it becomes
newly visible. Even, perhaps, complete.

## EACH OF US IN THE DOORWAY OF OURSELVES

The sky held and withheld yellow
like somebody braiding the hair of a restless
child. These days leaves fall so wet with last night's rain,
they drop to the place beneath as if it had been waiting
all year to embrace them. Yellow, in pieces,
all over the place, throat

of the bird we left on the railing
for days because it was too beautiful
to bury, until we woke to a halo of feathers
where bird had been. I thought of teeth then,
small, sharp, crunching the dark, and could hardly
do it, imagine biting into
what I'd forgotten was meat.

This was how the bird returned
to the living, transformed
into somebody else. It happens
all the time.

Not long ago,
I spotted a wedge of feathers behind a branch.
I had to invent the quick hook of the hawk's beak
smoothing, shaping delicate filaments
with its tip of sharpened spear—and then I remembered
the woman in line at the store
explaining the variety of piercings the skin can take.
She glittered with metals, her body a kind of warning.
I imagined tears slipping between the bright

studs but she wasn't crying. Something else, last night, three cries,
each high and gilded with pain. Something dying
out in the dark and what could I do? Unarmored, obscure
in the late hour when the edges of doing
and undoing seep together. All I could see was the guy
on his bike from the day before, bouncing
off the back of a car, how I stopped to stop time,
to watch him unfold from the floor of the road
and look for some kind of sign. Blurred, shrugging
his shoulders like feathered bundles
that collide with what still might be sky.

IMMORTALS

I need to stop trying
to leave the body behind,
its disappointments,
the skin more speckled than it used to be, the lines
more complicated. Descending the canyon, my knees
trembled like a couple of shivering dogs.
*Easy, now... there.* There. I wanted to go on, and on
where the stone held out its cupped hands,
where the sky, falling, had worn away
each curve. All of it perfectly
still. The great body of rock—
for once *beautiful* wasn't fleeting.

Light traveled down stone flanks each day,
broad hands, fingertips
then back up the other side of canyon walls
with their serious paint, their sorrow, their tapestries of stain.

I wanted their cups and hollows. Their rooms
within rooms. Mouths. Nostrils. Apertures of *almost*

whose silences were absolute.

Everywhere we clambered over rubble.
Enormous shelves, cracked away. Dissolving clots
of sand. Trees yanked and twisted under.
The night it rained I finally understood
not just disaster, but everything trickling down.
The streaked awnings of rock. The glorious. The ancient decay.

Leaving, I touched the last wall. I put my hand
into its shallow mouth, a bowl of sand. It held
its own disintegration. Itself within itself.

The sand was soft, and cool. I ruffled it.
I pressed my fingers down. I left that print behind
and then I climbed, my face dust-

streaked

this bundle of pieces still working together.
I climbed out into myself.
Into the cab of the pickup truck, the seat too big, my feet
sticking out like a kid's.
Stone ribs broke the surface of land
again and again, the road stretched thin, until
black cows lifted
out of nowhere, chewing, flicking their ears over new calves.

There's no stopping.
Here's my bag of raisins. My notebook, my pen.
The enormous wheels gripping the culverts, the birds
that seem to leap away, not fly.
Here is the rope, the cup, the box of bandaids:
my fortunes, arrayed. The book of chants,
the book, the chants, the last few notes I keep humming
under this
breath.

# FOUR — THE LOWER WING

# NET, SORROW, CRADLE

This was the day we had to go back into the world
with nothing, not even a bag of popcorn, not even
the ashes that would come to us later.
This was the day we had to buy breakfast, Sunday brunch
at a roadside family restaurant.
We were still among the living.

We had bodies we needed to feed
whether or not they remembered to hunger.

This was the day of the strangeness
of napkins and plates and hash-browned potatoes
spoons and forks awkward to hold, to handle
under the voices of angels blown inside-out,
the wind, shutters and curtains of
time closing behind us. Snap. Snap.

Oh heap of nothing—father, husband, brother, son.

      How do we ever go on?
How do we go back to singing?

When I see another grieving
now, I know
whatever lives below the throat, call it heart, call it howl,
call it wide-eyed stone—it drops
again, into that old sling, yes, still waiting
net, sorrow, cradle
riddled with holes, not falling, just
swaying above the abyss.

WHISTLING BEETHOVEN

At the corner of coming and going a man holds a scribbled sign
in the fist of wind. His coat accumulates
what blows, makes him a figure of leaves.
If you offer him a quarter and three foil-wrapped
sweets, he's quick to take them, already
unwrapping the chocolates, scarfing them down.
How the intersection roars
with the sound of his cells
rushing to live on anything, the swallowed
drop of the single coin into his empty pocket
is the silence of my father coming back in dreams,
his face not quite his face, his mouth
not quite saying
*don't wish the dead to return*
*when they've gone underneath tomorrow.*
                                  But today,
the rustling wind is pouring with sound,
with leaves, an entire Beethoven piano concerto
filling a faraway house. In the kitchen of yesterday
dinner is done and my father's up to his elbows in dishes.
He's whistling. He's plunging in with soapy hands,
the music a sea of whatever he didn't say,
and I want to call out
but the music keeps on playing. I can only step up
to my own sink, start to
whistle where he left off and imagine
feeding thick sandwiches
to the man at the corner no longer there.


I never knew
I knew the tune so well.

## IN THE MIDDLE OF SINGING

*I wish I had something warm to give you*
I said, but my pockets were empty.

And then the light changed.
*Maybe you could give me next summer* he called
as I cycled away. What did he mean?
An armful of sun right now, or fortitude
to last another season?

The mind invents new heat and leaves
from whatever it remembers, futures
put together from handfuls of the past

so the buck up the hill
antlers knocking and cracking
as he pulls lichen from empty branches
becomes a tree twisting free of the forest

becomes the boy that man might once have been,
and a friend, waving sticks, not minding the cold,
bright with the clack and impact of anything
that could make them large.

Remember the frogs in the blackberry vines
last September? Where the berries
were thick and fragrant and lost men slept
almost unnoticed.

## AROUND THE WORLD

When I heard they were aiming
to sail, I thought: fifteen months.
That's a long time to be on a boat.
And across the Pacific—how many days with no land?
But this is the feat: the immensity
of circling the globe
being, in the end, intensely private.

Maybe you brush up against the flank
of some continent, you see people
living their everyday extraordinary lives,
washing the street in front of a shop, spreading
seaweed over the rocks to dry.
You alight a minute, and then you simply
go on

the sea heaving, the wind becoming
so changeably precise. The longing, day after day,
to see whales, breathing, nearby. And how often,
really, do they surface? Isn't most of life hoping

to be close to some miracle,
its surprise?—the soft body
of the dead mole by the side of the road
I saw so briefly, riding by. Lying on its back,
muffled belly, the naked paws of digging
held open to bare light, and the sun spreading its
long fingers everywhere, rubbing in
that final gold.  Or when I saw Mr. Cole
stopping by his mailbox, I waited at the bottom of the hill—
I don't know why—as he opened
his car door and climbed out, slowly,

his eyes finding level. He moved around the front of the car
like a tipped tree
carrying an invisible accumulation of snow
on his shoulders, finding the ground with each step
as if his feet were remembering
a poem he'd learned by heart
seventy years ago, as if he were practicing
walking across the surface
of an imagined sea.

## MUSEUM OF ART

Wading girl up to her knees, leaping
dog suspended over water, a scattering
of caught
droplets

> *Do you have a favorite part of the museum?* I asked the guard.
> Nobody else was there.

Faraway on a sun bright swing
under a bridge blocking most of the sky

> The question seemed to take him
> by surprise.

Ice horse, somewhere in Siberia,
sad gaze, a rhinoceros

> He fell
> from the invisible pose
> of the invisible. But stayed guarded.

Beached whales, the surf pink,
sand, sky. Curves where everything met

> *I don't know.* He shrugged. *Exhibits change...*

Paintings of empty rooms, a wall

> I thought that was that, but it wasn't.
> *Works I especially like,*
> *they change, too*

Open window, one curtain, billow
of painted wind

> *Today, I'd say one or two downstairs...*

Ancient gift baskets, woven, feathered

He didn't say which ones.
*There are also paintings I don't like. Then*
*they grow on me.*

Colored glass on a fluted stem

*Actually, you know what?*
*When you spend a long time looking at something, it changes.*

Two stone figures: rib bones, spines just visible,
ladders up the center of
some previous eternity

*In this job you spend a lot of time with nothing to do but look.*

Carved woman, a child on her hip,
his face blank with weariness, her face
blank with weariness

*You look long enough, you realize*
*something there is alive. I think*
*Art is alive.*

Red paint, alone. Dancing
mask wanting holy eagle down
to float, float free

*Or maybe.*
*I'm the one who changes. Maybe I'm the one*
*alive.*

We waited there.

Afternoon, two rowers, rowing into blue
and gold

*Try to see the lower wing,* he said.

## BEYOND SWANS

My friend once ate a swan,
the only thing she was ashamed to admit
she'd gladly eat again. She said
it tasted like nothing else,

more like eating a god, I thought,
sky god, cloud god, thunderbolts fallen
from its now slack beak. The body come
plummeting down, or pulled from the water:
a huge feathered bugle curved upon itself,
waiting for breath to sound it. How could you

carry all that silent whiteness home?
The intimacy of weight
lighter, and heavier, than expected. The head
draped over your shoulder, soft as a child's,
bobbing a little as children do when they fall asleep
in your arms as you walk down a long path,
the sky closing and seeming to detach
from gravity the way the body does
falling into sleep. I remember

almost sleeping in my father's arms
late at night after the bonfire, by the sea,
after the tide had returned.
He climbed up and over rocks,
and my body felt loose and safe:
almost asleep being almost innocence,
but awake enough to feel
my own limp feet sway,
to feel how gently he carried me.

This is how I'd carry her,
the one-who-ate-a-swan, who probably
never will again, whose burdens now
have changed their shapes, as burdens do.
And this is how it goes: the lake
a long way from anywhere and night
already approaching, the uneven ground
stumbling a little beneath you, then rising
to meet you again, your load, a heavy cloud,
plucked from clouds, becoming more and more
indistinguishable from whatever you thought you were
as the gray edge recedes into dusk.

## POST OFFICE IN DECEMBER

Everyone stands and waits, I want to say
*like a field of cows* but you can't compare people to cows
kindly, even when you're thinking of steadiness,
a patient way one might contemplate,
jaw rocking like the sea and faraway eyes
full of private anthems. Today,
everyone's pregnant with packages and stacks of cards
as the postman nudges his reluctant machine.
Any questions? he asks the quiet room
and someone says *Do you think my brother'll like
what I've got in here?*
The postman laughs, and taps another key.

The man in line behind me opens a book
small, red and black, like a piece of ancient
pottery and offers to read me a poem
about the man who built the Trojan horse.
The builder my reader recounts wasn't thinking
about horses or the magnificence of limbs
or the charm and doom of unsuspected rooms within.
It was a job to get done: Lengths of board. Number of nails.
How to make it fit together. How to make it sound.
The man looks up. Shrugs.
*I guess there are always people like that* he says

and waves at a woman who turns and smiles
like someone you wake incompletely
from a complicated dream.
She's come to pick up the hot pink horse blanket
she ordered for the pony grown too old
to handle winters further east. She hopes
the horse will be happy here and will get on well
with her field of rescued cows.

It all makes sense somehow. I want to drive out
in search of wet grass, cows, a distant point of pink.
The rain is cold. It might turn to snow.
The parking lot rises in little plumes, people
breathing their way in, and out. The sky a rolling horse
its feet somewhere in the clouds—how did I never see it before?
—that dark mane of Douglas fir, the elegant arch of neck
and all of us inside it.

## IN THE BRIEF KINGDOM OF ICE

In the clearing above us
    bundled families
pulled wide-eyed children on plastic sleds.
They were laughing, snapping photos
    in that new way new parents have

when you can hold the world by the hand

as it licks a slanted windowpane of ice
with a small pink
    question mark of tongue.

Time circled them all like a puppy

as we entered the crashing forest
    my sons and I,
ducking past the glass gate of toppled branches
icicles rising like extinguished candles
from arms twisted upside-down.

Under trees falling around us
we crunched through the rush
of letting go—
great limbs cracking, plummeting
—a gash of weight
then nothing.

The heart drops, then resumes,
perfumed in piney confusion
of green and dying.

But in this shatter—
didn't we feel alive together? Each step
on the edge of glory and disaster.

Everything wet and glittering.
    Everything going, fast.

## SOME WINTER

I watched an old man today ease himself into a chair
as if he were made of snow,
the kind that barely sticks together
although you want to build
        out of pure white again
snowballs and forts
        with everyone pink-faced and panting—

but this old man snow is dry and loose
a handful of dust—
        the snowball will last
only as long as you cup your hands around it

and suddenly I knew: I will not live
        to see my sons grow elderly.

They'll have to do it on their own,
carrying their paper plates to the next empty chair.

        If I could comfort them then—

When the first was born, fierce and
fragile, I'd wake startled from any sleep, thinking:
        *He is here! He is still here!*
And I'd go and look to be sure—and there he was,
still real.

When they are old men I won't know what real is.

I'd come back if I could—
        just to adore them, gaze upon their wrinkled faces,
their rheumy eyes
looking to the windows, the snow thicker now
coming in fat bunches
        like sweet ripe fruit—if only
we could climb out onto the roof like we used to
up where the grapes grow ripest
        the snow licking us rosy
        in all its wet tongues.

## SWING SONG

The afternoon floated down around us.
My son flew into the warm air
And I felt forever linger
Somewhere between leaf-light and swing.

My son flew into the warm air,
His hair floating up
Somewhere between leaf-light and swing
He looked like I once did.

His hair floating up
Every time the swing came back
He looked like I once did
In a reverie of trees.

Every time the swing came back
I sent him out again
In a reverie of trees
How he flew and returned! Flew and returned.

I sent him out again
To the sound of distant children
How he flew and returned, flew and returned
Quicksilver child in one quiet arc

To the sound of distant children
The afternoon floated down around us
Quicksilver child in one quiet arc
I felt forever linger.

LETTING GO

I would cradle your head in my arms
but a bear no one sees
pins my hands between its teeth.
The birds are singing over and over
behind my eyes. I have folded your hair
in a little shroud. I have unbuttoned
all the books we once read. I have collected
cups of rainwater from the corners
of yesterday, and now I am measuring
your long long shadow as it stretches into limbs
of light and shade. I am trying to open
the windows as far as they will swing
for the air to come in
and the air to go out again,
for the sun to rise and set, for your bright
sailing away.

ABATEMENT

*...the abatement contractor will be here Monday to start the abatement process of removing the decrepit storage building.... —Facilities Manager*


Today is Monday and the white-crowned sparrow
lets loose another song washed and salted
by wind above the space that was a house.

This is how you unmake unmaking:

Take the patch of grass between the stand
of brushy trees and weedy creek, the unmown sweep
beside the house that was a house. A child
wades through green, and green
the sun has lit all blades to blazing
as the child pulls galls from leaves of alders
because such oddity must be magic.
Pages with nothing on them
have something *in* them: bead, berry, bud, bump.
She wraps them in her shirt.
She'll decide what to call them, later.

Home is what you hear when you are dreamy, when
the olive-sided flycatcher quivers at the tip of extremity
and calls out, once, twice, and falls
to pluck its sustenance from air. And the wind
caroms off the dangling ropes of the boats in their harbor
and the fishermen climb ashore, and the gulls
scream their arias of appetite.

The child has gone inside, bare floors creaking, kittens
mewling from the nest of blankets on the bed.
See how the rooms half-close
their eyes? Little ghosts nursing in the shadows.
She knows things we can't
remember in the rooms of her early-morning mind,
her hair still warm from standing in the sun.

And under all that came between
that house and now,
a symphony of things, rising from the rubble:
wet shoes left on the porch all night.
Piles of broken shells and the sound they make,
rubbed together, or shaken, softly. The persistence of wind.
Rain, sometimes saying things,

and the first honey scent of sand verbena in an empty lot.
Imagine your face so close to fragrance,
precise and many-cupped, nestled there,
dry sand sticks to your cheek
and the wind
bellows by without ever touching your skin.

## SOUNDING

And now, the green and yellow chorus
from all the stations of the trees
above the farther rumble of the highway.
That dull growl travels miles
from the lines it traces. Just yesterday
on the way to buy another fence,
I heard something called *music of distance*
playing on the radio, and visualized nothing.
Just sound, vibrating
like a room made of rain.

I didn't want to hear it. Didn't want to go
falling into emptiness again
just as I didn't want to read about more killing,
its terrible unfolding and the long moment
before it stills. When I tried to describe
the voice of Dylan Thomas
I thought of a swinging pendulum,
an oracle speaking from the bottom of a well.
But there was also a many-layered
psalm to everyday, its peculiar rhythm
residing in some long-suspended moment
after a war, in late spring, nearly

summer, like the hour the bear swayed through
the uncut grass to swipe a pawful of eggs from the coop.
She left a trail of eggshells and feathers, breaking
the little hen almost before it could give voice
to wanting to wake from the terrible dream
and stay a little longer.
But it wasn't that time, no, it was the next, when the first fence
stood ready, and the bear came again—and felt the sting
and clatter of charge charging through—
not the long drawn current of moving water, but the wild snap

you hear where the trail dips under power lines:
the hiss and crackle as spaces make
and unmake themselves—and in the midnight heat
the bellow, and moan, a shape
forming out of sound.

If the bear's been back a third time,
I haven't seen her. No more than I've seen
a man about to die a horrible death, and keep seeing it
whenever I remember what I read—yesterday I had to buy milk
and carrots, and the checkout line was full of sensational news:
people I didn't know torn apart by ruined beauty.
*Why didn't the hero just turn around*
*and walk back the way he came?* a boy once asked
in the middle of a story.
*A person hardly ever walks in a straight line,* I said.
All kinds of things can throw you. The wind pushes
from the side, and you keep brushing your hair out of your face.
One hip, a little stiff and you end up

not where you expected. What happened to breakfasts?
When she talked, my grandmother's tangents grew so long
she forgot what got her started. That's what she said:
*now, what got me started?*—with a cut square of barely buttered toast
held halfway to her lips.

FLOAT

Where the creek widened between the trees,
the sun stilled, floating, as we were
floating, as if we'd found a room where
the light pooled, where you couldn't hear
the traffic anymore, and the train's long
racket had long since gone.

Here the current dozes, wind does not touch down.
Before, it ran in trees above us, the clatter
of branches knocking branches overhead—there's always
a little breakage going on, a little crashing

—but now the birds go dipping through those green
limbs, and who would have thought *dipping*
could be so beautiful a word?—and isn't it?—
a dipper, that which enters below
so easily, so simply, you almost forget
it didn't always belong.

It's like taking a breath, maybe you close
your mouth, your eyes and then you sink
into the other green beneath you, and let it close
for a moment, over the top of your head—

Now the smallest sounds riffle and stir.
A rustle. A soft gulping from under the leaves.

And when the dipper lifts, dripping, and full
of what it entered, it comes back to us
with some of that other world which can only be held
if you hold yourself like a bowl.

We float under the long bare arms of the sun, not moving.
The shape of a fish glides
under the creek's gilded skin. Pollen and seed-fluff
riding the sheen.
It takes time, not moving, to see the reeds
that rise from the edge of the creek
shift and wobble. Not in the wind that has left us,
not in the current, which has stilled.
We watch those grasses undulate, pushed
by whatever swims among them,
by whatever can't know
how the green stems give them away.

## IT'S BEEN A LONG TIME SINCE
## I TALKED WITH A MOUNTAIN

My mother dozes off in her chair because it is late
and the fire is warm and her new fiancé
nods in his sweater
and matching brown socks. Light quivers
in what still fills a glass on the table beside her, another moment
we might paste in a book to look at later and sigh
because we can see on the page what, by then,
has gone: this firelight's sleepy heat, the nearness of these people
residing each in their own unraveling stories,
climbing the rafters of sleep into private, flickering worlds—
and watching them dream, I realize
it's been a long time since I talked with a mountain

heard that high thin wind filtering over and through
flaking rock and the tiny faces of alpine blooms,
the wild hair tassels of seeds. Years ago we nearly missed the top
of a mountain pass, stopped by members of that other party
rushing down in help or hope or helplessness
as a man lay dying on the trail above. They motioned us to wait
and we sat, little family, by the side of the line of earth we'd followed.
Dust became apparent on our legs. The sun curved its gleaming hand
to make white spirits dance from the face of a watch
onto a tangle of leaves. Here the scent
of dry and gathered sweat, and silence,
marked by the footprints of ants, a beetle meandering under a stick
and the dying man just beyond us in the dappling of firs.
When they carried him down in the privacy of grief
we looked away. We stood as trees would, alive and still, reaching
into light's long wordless sleeve.

And then we went on. We had to,
didn't we? Up to the crest of wildflowers and streams,
mountain goats and marmots, a brief Eden nestled
beneath the sky. We hardly spoke. Each of us carried
something fragile and unwieldy, into which every breath
disappears. This was our last hike. Did we feel it then,
without a name? Shaking the air
so slightly? A coolness on the skin that always comes
when you stop for a moment after a climb. The sky,
higher than mountains, comes down to our feet.
It is what we always step through.

BLOOMING

Bird, come hop over me, four times.
So that after I fool myself into dying I can get up again,
go on my way as if the sky had simply passed
behind a passing notion.

It took a while, but I finally saw a body
moving in the tree.
Small bird person, busy with her own life.
This is as it should be. Branches
wobbling, air
not yet warm, but lit by cherry blossoms.

Only—she's not a bird person, this one, she's a tassel
of fur: chipmunk, chatter, a faceful of flowers.
Quivering.
Everything secretly sweet. Everything eating
and also something to eat.

Life goes in and out of itself.
We could count the openings.
Not all these blooming branches are attached.
Some, loose, have been held in the air
by those on which they fell.
They open anyhow.
The chipmunk teeters on oscillations
of plumy white. Steals fruit before it's fruit.
Before it isn't.

And this whole day belongs to anyone who takes it,
harvesters of petals, teeth, sweet swallow of
any kind of blooming.

# NOTES

"Canyon del Muerto" is after a photograph with the same name by Gary Tepfer.

"Goodnight Gorilla" responds to an event occurring on October 18, 2011, when Terry Thompson released 56 exotic animals from his Muskingum County Animal Farm before shooting himself in the head. In an effort to protect the public, the police shot and killed 49 of the animals roaming Zanesville, OH. The title is taken from *Goodnight Gorilla*, a picture book by Peggy Rathmann.

# ACKNOWLEDGMENTS

My thanks to the editors of the following magazines in which versions of some of these poems previously appeared.

*The Inflectionist Review*, "Almost Venice" and "When the nth Term Is Infinite" (under the title "Where the Muses"), "Under My Pillow"

*Cider Press Review*, "Goodnight Gorilla" (under the title "Elegy")

*Tor House Review*, "Strange Coat" (under the title "What We Don't See")

*Prairie Schooner,* "It's Been a Long Time Since I Talked With a Mountain"

*South Carolina Review*, "Post Office in December"

*Carapace,* "Swing Song"

*Hubbub,* "Around the World"

*Comstock Review,* "Incoming," "What if," "Whistling Beethoven," "In the Middle of Singing"

*Poetry City,* "Beyond Swans"

*Gyroscope Review,* "Handkerchief," "My Mother's Fox"

*Paterson Literary Review,* "Some Winter"

*december magazine,* "Wet Horses"

*Paper Nautilus,* "Gift Horse" (under the title "No So What")

# THANKS

Forever thanks to Leo for always being there.

To Jacob and Eli, who have filled and keep filling so many buckets of my life.

To my mother, for her celebration of all I do.

To Maxine Scates, for her passion and inspiration.

To my poet friends in abundance, especially those of poetry breakfasts, Wednesday night workshops, Poetry 1 gatherings, and Waywords, for their support, advice and helpful perspective.

To the Airlie folk: Deb Akers, Darlene Pagan, Karen McPherson, Tim Shaner, Tim Whitsel, Jon Boisvert, and Tola Molotkov, for embracing this collection and bringing it to fruition.

To Beth Ford for her thoughtful consideration of how to build the best boat for these particular poems.

## ABOUT THE PUBLISHER

Airlie Press is run by writers. A nonprofit publishing collective, the press is dedicated to producing beautiful and compelling books of poetry. Its mission is to offer a shared-work publishing alternative for writers working in the Pacific Northwest. Airlie Press is supported by book sales and donations. All funds return to the press for the creation of new books of poetry.

## COLOPHON

The titles and poems are set in Mrs. Eaves Roman. This typeface is named after Sarah Eaves, the woman who became John Baskerville's wife. As Baskerville was setting up his printing and type business, Mrs. Eaves moved in with him as a live-in housekeeper, eventually becoming his wife after the death of her first husband, Mr. Eaves. Like the widows of Caslon, Bodoni, and the daughters of Fournier, Sarah similarly completed the printing of the unfinished volumes that John Baskerville left upon his death.